LOST ORIGINALS

BOOKS BY IRVING FELDMAN

LOST ORIGINALS

POEMS BY

IRVING FELDMAN

HOLT, RINEHART AND WINSTON

CHICAGO   NEW YORK   SAN FRANCISCO

"As Fast as You Can" was first published in *New American Review* *#11;* "The Titanic" and "My Olson Elegy" in *New American Review* *#12;* "After the Flight from Rockaway" in *The New Yorker;* "The Jumping Children" in *Michigan Quarterly Review;* "The Tenor" in *Modern Occasions;* "The Party" and "Birthday" in *Columbia Forum;* "A Balcony in Barcelona" (part 2) in *Salmagundi;* "A Balcony in Barcelona" (part 1) and "The Air Children" in *The Nation;* "The Apocalypse Is a School for Prophets" in *Midstream;* and "So It Happens" in *Choice,* a magazine of poetry.

The author wishes to express his gratitude to the Research Foundation of the State University of New York for a grant enabling him to complete this work.

TO SARAH & RUTH & CHICK

CONTENTS

LOST ORIGINALS

Loosed from the shaping hand, who lay
at the window, face to the open sky,
the fever of birth now cooling, cooling?
I! said the gingerbread man leaping
upright laughing; the first faint dawn
of breath roared in his lungs and toes; down
he jumped running.

Sweet was the dream
of speed that sped the ground under, sweet
the ease of this breathing, which ran
in his body as he now ran in the wind,
leaf in the world's breathing; sweeter still
the risk he was running: of boundaries first
and then the unbounded, a murderous
roadway that ended nowhere in trees,
a cat at creamspill looking up, mysterious
schoolboys grabbing.

(Certainly, they saw him,
a plump figure hurrying, garbed in three
white buttons, edible boots, his head a hat
in two dimensions.)

Powerfully then
his rhythmic running overtook the dream
of his flight: he was only his breathing.
He said, entering his body, *Like this
I can go on forever.*

Loping and leaping
the fox kept pace, hinted, feinting, over

and under wherever, licking his chops
and grinning to the hilt of his healthy gums.
Breathing to his toes the man ran faster,
free in a world that was suddenly growing
a bushy tail and a way of its own.
No less his joy for the darkening race!
Brilliant thought had dawned to his lips;
he understood it: Thrilling absolute
of original breath! and said, *The world
desires me! Somebody wants to eat me up!*
That stride transported flying him off
earth and mystic into the fox's maw
blazing. One with the world's danger
that now is nothingness and now a tooth,
he transcended the matter of bread.
His speed between the clickers was infinite.

Tell them this, that life is sweet!
eagerly he told the happy fox
whose pink tongue assenting glibly
assuaged the pure delirious crumbs.
(Others fable otherwise, of course:
Having outsped our sight, he dazzles
the spinning heavens, that fox our senses'
starved pretention. How else explain
the world's ubiquitous odor
of sweetness burning and the absence of ash?)

Shimmering and redolent, his spirit
tempts our subtlest appetite. There he runs!
freely on the wind. We sniff a sharp
intelligence, lunge and snap our teeth
at the breathable body of air
and murmur while it is flying by,
Life is unhappy, life is sweet!

Secret in a woman's coat, her hat,
his face hidden by a veil, crazy
with fear and shame there among women
and children shivering in the boat,
he escaped huddled over an oar
on the cold and coldly misted sea.
His last sight was the deck awash and screaming.
Sick to the depths of his stomach,
he retched on the gray Newfoundland shore
and drowned in the bitter syncope.
Under a hovel roof, he woke
naked in a woman's arms and could
remember nothing, having become
what henceforth he would call *himself*.

One hundred fathoms down, withdrawn
from every future and larger than life,
with nothing left to lose or wish, the Titans
sit in their eternal afterglow
and with glorious instruments—
curving, belled, and fluted, the fruits
of a golden age—blow upward,
in vast unison and bubbling serenity,
toward the solemn void, the dizzying precipice,
God Save the King!

MY OLSON ELEGY

I set out now
in a box upon the sea. Maximus VI

Three weeks, and now I hear!
What a headstart for the other elegists!
I say, No matter! by any route and manner
we shall arrive beside you together.
Envy, Triumph, Pride, Derision:
such passionate oarsmen drive my harpooneer,
he hurls himself through your side.
You lie and wait to be overtaken.
You absent yourself at every touch.

It was an adolescent, a poetboy,
who told me—one of that species, spoiled,
self-showing, noisy, conceited, *épatants*,—
voice breaking from the ego-distance like
a telephone's, not a voice indeed
but one in facsimile, recon-
stituted static, a locust voice,
exhumed, resurrected, chirring
in its seventeenth year, contentedly
saying, "And I've just completed
section fifteen of my Olson elegy."

Landscape on legs, old Niagara!—all
the unique force, the common vacancy,
the silence and seaward tumultuous gorge
slowly clogging with your own *disjecta*,
tourists, trivia, history,
disciples, picnickers in hell;
oh great Derivative in quest

of your own unknown author, the source,
a flying bit of the beginning blast,
sky-shard where early thunder slumbers:
the first syllabic grunt, a danger,
a nameless name, a tap on the head; you,
Olson!, whale, thrasher, bard of bigthink,
your cargo of ambergris and pain,
your steamy stupendous sputtering
—all apocalypse and no end:
precocious larvae have begun to try
the collected works beneath your battered sides.

See them now! dazzling elegists sitting
on their silvery kites on air
like symbols in flight, swooping daredevils
jockey for position, mount a hasty breeze
and come careering at your vastness
to tread among the gulls and plover
—but the natural cries of birds do not
console us for our gift of speech.
Embarrassed before the sea and silence,
we do not rise or sing,
wherefore this choir of eternal boys
strut and sigh and puff their chests and stare
outward from the foundering beach.

King of the flowering deathboat, falls,
island, leviathan, starship night,
you plunge to the primitive deep
where satire's puny dreadful monsters,
its Follies and its Vices, cannot reach,
and swim among their lost originals
—free, forgotten, powerful, moving
wholly in a universe of rhythm—
and re-enter your own first Fool,

inventing happiness out of nothing.
You are the legend death and the sea have seized
in order to become explicable.

—Smell of salt is everywhere,
speed and space burn monstrousness
away, exaltation blooms in the clear:
fair weather, great *bonanza*, the high!,
swelling treasure, blue catch of heaven.
The swimmer like the sea reaches every shore.
Superlative song levitates from lips
of the glowing memorialists,
their selves flash upward in the sun.

Now you are heavier than earth, everything
has become lighter than the air.

Arriving at last, he threw down the burden from
his back, his hump, the mailpouch his father.
Well, he thought, straightening, *these* letters
will never be delivered, unless themselves they go.
As if in answer, glittering and quick,
as white as milk, the ancient promises dove
into the pores of the ground.
                              Hump stayed put,
fuddle-fardel changed and changing.
It made him laugh and weep to see
his heap: marvelous callosity
of passed possibles and plenty's
opalescent horn, the little fluxflocks,
oh made him weep and cheer to hear
love's lithe youngtongue's shaping song

mouthoozemuse
titwitwoostalk
stablebabelburble
mamadrama
murmur-butt
plum plump lump bump
mud-udder
underhump of moo-maid
clod of milkmud, of claycud
tongue of muddlemodeler spoon and spade
babyshape
so tender to touch: smother sup
sleeperslupper
bloomballoomboom
sayseedsomescatterthing
thunder lung

a ling a ling am
goat goad 'em scrotum
god prod in pod
rosey ring
hole hilly high light
skyskullscald
and down fall all!
humpty-thump in sulph-muddlepuddle
                    in self-meddlepedal
                    in silt-middlepiddle
dauphin-coffin
tumblestone and rubblebone
· apocalumps
all out! all off!
and all groan up!
                    Last leaped forth
leathery, wizened-wise, he, Humpback self,
and stood curved, panting before him as if
from long labor, then stoopingly strutted,
confronted, while himself tender touching
and frotting a bald spot frayed on his back.
He saw the Hunch was tiny as a child,
aged as a sire, cackling as a goose, crackling
as fire, tricky as trouble is was he,
manjock grizzled, fizzled, fiercer-farcer,
stick stuck in earth, bent body C,
and held a bag of pennies, held a key.

So that is what you look like, he addressed
the humped one. Who are you? My father are you?

You who are, impostor?
What have done with son,
child of dreams, child I would have been?

Father, he I am, that very child!

Then I'll eat you up, you worstwurst, you father
-fodder, huffed the gnome, puffing and swelling
and showing the sharkshead that grew from his back.
For I am thy father-farter, thy thunder-thudder!

Eh? Say again! I dare.

         I am die fudder
-flooder, die dunder-dudder, die blooder!

And my sputter spitter! How could runt you
eat me giant? he asked his father.

If no respect, no, oh pity then me
who need a thousand years to straighten back,
so long have bent at dismal diking,
abandoned, alone, and none relieves,
bitter nights bright days, wanting wee,
waters within, without, withholding.

Not shamed you seen such bad posture?

Now tears he could not withhold.
Many they were, obedient to gravity.
O better I had never been born!,
bitter I niver bin bone, 'lone and muvverless on erf!
His numbed lips could scarcely make the sounds.

If father curses life, what shall son say?
Nothing. So said he it ever and ever.
But hunchback held not his peace:
Pursuing future, dreaming self,

half of you has been desire,
other half, conceit,
but desire does not savor always,
sweet conceit sours in its season.
Bitter bastard, do not deny me, do not
refuse my legacy! I am your father
and your father's fathers. I am your key,
crouch on my here heap, this hump
of refuse, wreckage, scurf. Moriah my.
Foresee I promised earth, son and city. Way
is narrow, is hard, passage difficult,
wince will you going through. Go, too, I
may not, help shall, save you maybe,
am key.

He touched the hunchback's back and found it ridged
like the frozen sea. Indeed, he was the key.
Quickly he turned him in the lock then.
Key melted, and hump broke
and stone broke, the river ran by.
Briefly he saw blue eyes bubbled, floating
on the water, their gaze of pain, puzzlement,
eternal shyness too too much to say goodbye.
And wild water's mouth sucking itself down, drowning,
shouted, Save yourself, you sonofabitch,
but save me too, save our family, our history!

Stooping he drank the knowledge that flowed
at his feet like a mountain stream, so cold,
so strong, so pure it humbled and broke his mouth,
stung his ears and stopped his heart
like sentence of death: the taste
beyond spitting out, extenuation,
of his unmitigable mediocrity.

He knew then he was not free,
but of what he was not knew not,
nor to what end or why.

The field is lively with children. Although it is
night and sleep is commanded, they are
awake, linked perhaps in secret to the
antipodes, the day. Dressed in the styles of
forty years ago, like discontinued angels,
they do not move forward or back, they are
jumping, crying as they rise, I want to be, I
bet myself!, singing as they sink, I am my
point of repose, no other.

These, who have just begun to master the
simultaneous leaping and wing-beating,
repeat their abrupt impromptu floppings like
dancers warming up who take off without
apparent cues, collapse before completing
the arc; while others, as if testing the ground
underfoot, hop a bare bit, never exceed the
measure, come down with patient zeal.
Some here, thrusting with flutter kicks, jump
higher and higher, bounding up in great
leaps, their little throats swell like gulls', they
soar and sing. The joy in descent is no less
than the leaping, their concentration is
absolute, their fall is flying. Afoot, they lift
their knees like runners after a race,
half-bend from the waist, and windily shake
their dusty cloth wings on the clattering
wire frames.
The cripples with withered legs, with powerful
crutch-wielding shoulders, who—if they
were actual children—would have scuttled
after the crowd of racers, one side dragging,
the other leaping forward, jump now in

eager hobbled verticals, balancing on
useless legs until their arms take hold and
lift them from deformity.
The children with the largest pinions leap
lowest, endure longest, appear in their
endless hovering hardly to move at all,
comets whose flight so far exceeds a lifetime
they seem never to absent the sky, as
though they attended an unending
revelation.
These others flex knees and drone until
their heads reverberate with the sound of
motor flight, suddenly their chests'
marvelous din lifts them before their legs
can spring.
Unaware of the power of fragility, little
hunchbacks, with their mysterious
conformity to invisible circumstances,
crouch and hop on one leg only.

Jumping is a pleasure, a mystery. And it is
exciting to be among so many. Breathing
the space, they refine themselves, each
becomes his single substance. Straining, he
leaps, his leap overcomes him, jumping
lightly on to his shoulders.
Now they are bounding in the beautiful dark
interim, eager to jump from the embrace of
your fantasy, to be actual children who
press bright bobbing faces against the high
windows and peer into the darkened room,
where you lie in bed imagining their
ebullient society. Even now, they crowd the
street at your door, call you out with
irresistible greetings.

If Eden ever was, it cannot now
be seen, obscured by what is certain:
the treasure of our wakefulness,
its aura we have called the day,
these vivid shards we dream are daggers,
these dreams we strike against the dark,
a vastness of slivers outshining
the plainness, the clarity,
the pleasure of Eden.

Gazing deeply at, but never into,
the bright impenetrable bits, too densely
bright, we cannot enter, cannot break
them smaller—our gaze is halted by
their perfect whiteness of frozen fire—
we sense the pain of their cramming in,
immurement, of, then, their exudation,
as it seems, of light, how powerfully
they wish for wholeness now if only
in commingled radiance!—we sense
the pain of this desire, of all desire,
we feel their kinship to us, we say,
The day was made for us, we are the day.

No farther on we see, no farther back,
our blindness, the visible world concur:
nullity of everything less brilliant than
these shatterings of our lost terror
—the flaming swords of those gods those heroes
who, desiring us and our desire, came
and burned Paradise to the ground.

Dying, Morton saw a child who was
the child he'd been, who would become
the man he is, now almost no longer
is—already the boy's shoulder had
huddled subtly forward as if it cradled
a heart-attack, some incurable effort
at perhaps an impossible freedom;
he seemed, bright against the subtracted
dark, to have banished every background.
Then Morton understood the missing world,
the hidden heart-attack were one.

Could he have stopped him, crying out,
"You, go back! for out of every
possibility, you alone will die?"
His throat was glued shut. The child
no less pursued him, loomed forward, soon
would be as large as he, soon be him.
Or would have waved him off . . . but the boy,
helpless or too resolved, made no sign,
did not stop. Then Morton touched crushed hand
to broken mouth and sucked the pain it held,
and huddled in mourning for the child—
father, son, himself, his heart, which?
—missing forever from Paradise.
Culpable, the bitterness of his shame
united with the mystery of death
in something he could only call hell.

Behind a high overshadowing wall, dark,
barred, forbidding—surely that is
Eden, he thought—he heard the creatures

he had refused to be, harelip, crocochild,
calf's head, lung, shy imperfect beasts,
carouse, thump, groan, mutter coarse
unwordable noises, strangled gutturals
that shuddered in him as if, deep within,
a giant hand were slamming doors.
He thought, If I could see them once again
I might not die. So great his yearning,
one door stayed open a crack, a slit . . .
quickly all of him slipped through.

1

Aboard the wreck, passengers crowded
the windows, peered out. And saw
a band of children struggling in the surge
of a purely green and sunlit field.
How amazing the field's swift flow
forward, and that children had appeared
plunging toward them at its farthest border!
And they, happy to forget their obvious
wounds, were thinking, So, we are wrecked
relative only to all the rest, with which
we no longer keep pace, no longer desire!
Forgive their error, they desired so much
—how else could they be dying?—and yes,
they heard far off the children courageously
singing Courage! to their reviving hearts.
See there! see there! they shouted inwardly,
each gesturing in his throat to a child
overwhelmed and farther off than ever
but pressing toward them with all its might.
Nonetheless, in thought at least and blindly,
they were leaping forward for the rope
the distant hands held out . . . leaping
for a point a world at last
without direction.

2

The children who came across the field
to gawk at the fabulous disaster
found it, toppled in a dry ravine,
its forwardness collapsed, its body
smashed open, rusted out, gutted;
inside it nothing, stale emptiness,
the smell of old air in a tire—unless
the little babble they thought they heard
was cries of children crying out, or beating
of something, a heart, hidden, marvelous.
Swiftly the marvel was disaster.
Within the wreck, a whirlwind
blew up their lungs,
and looking out they saw the pasture:
a garden of cut gestures, blown away,
crushed in the sudden distance
—little bridge, bright morning, themselves
standing there, dwindling
in the infinitesimal splendor,
a pinhole blazing lost light.
No star can bring it back!
At this speed, in this darkness, they know
they won't get out again, ever.

X

am I speaking to you
    yes

are you listening to me
    yes

what time is it
    it is too early to say

how early is that
    before the bird,
    before dawn

is it dark
    yes

what is that
    your breathing

and that silence
    that is silence

where was I
    with darkness, death
    far away

and how did I come here
    breathing,
    asking questions

is it still too early
    yes,
    I cannot say yet

why can't you say
    I must listen

ought I to be frightened
    no,
    you must not be frightened

shall I go on asking questions
    I cling to your voice

will that be very long
    yes,
    not longer than you can endure

and then what will happen
    I shall say you are my child,
    the dead will arise

at dawn
    at dawn

and will I have my things back
    I don't know

will I want them still
    I don't know

what were they
    your toys,
    your tribe

why did you give them away
    you were dying,
    I thought so

was that right of you
  wrong,
  bitterly wrong

did I cry
  I don't know

why do you say I don't know
  I don't know

are you being honest
  I don't know,
  no

what time is it now
  dark

and will I have children of my own
  they will be numberless,
  they will name you in their prayers

will I hear their prayers
  you will hear them
  listening for you

is that what you are doing now
  yes,
  I am praying

will you be my child
  yes,
  if I can

what is my name
  you will know it

will I remember that I was dead
    as in a dream
    only

where am I now
    near me,
    near my ear

am I as close as that
    yes,
    closer

but why am I dead
    I cannot say that

won't you tell
    I am afraid

did you kill me
    yes

were you alone
    yes,
    there were others

why don't you speak louder
    I am afraid

who were they
    very many

and am I alone
    no,
    you are many

who
 father
 fathers
 son
 sons
 brother
 brothers

why should I be born again
 I cannot live without you

are you also dead
 yes,
 I am dead

will you be born again
 I think so

are you me
 yes,
 also

will I have to stay a child
 I don't know,
 I don't think so

will I have a body then
 yes

where is my body now
 lying
 in a field
 on a hill
 near a tree

will I forgive you
    yes,
    I am unforgivable

why
    you will hear my prayer

and then I will assent
    I don't know
    I think so

why will I assent
    I don't know

and am I messiah
    yes

and messiah is a dead child
    yes,
    from the dead kingdom,
    hunting his children

and will I find them
    I don't know

and will I come to you at dawn
    promptly

and you will be here
    yes

and you will assent to my return
    I will try

and will you succeed
    if I hear the words

what are they
    I don't know,
    my words

what is assent
    my heart overflows

will my heart overflow
    with light,
    yes

may I sleep now until it is time
    I cannot endure
    not to hear you

will you continue to listen
    yes,
    that is my prayer

and you will hear
    breathing,
    you,
    I think

can you be more definite
    no

will you wake me in time

And arrives where all are strangers, all
are kind. He thinks, We are familiar, surely,
since they are kind, and yet seem strangers
—or I am someone other than I think,
myself the only stranger.

                      They come close
now with smiles and offerings, with large
sounds, with faces luminous and vague,
with gestures inviting one to sit down,
to dine, to take one's ease, to stay
among them or, if one chooses, to leave
in peace, but later, later on. He thinks
it endlessly, teasingly perplexing; he asks,
Whom do they find so lovable? Someone
they were awaiting? Am I that person?
And believes himself an impostor
imposing, a grabber of gifts intended
for others, but senses afterward
how impersonal their kindness, how
profound their courtesy, that they should
have greeted him as brightly had he been
any other.

              This is reposeful, a final
kindness, a tact, not to require response
and answers. If there was another life,
he hardly remembers it now, or if
he came this way on a particular
errand, and cannot declare for certain
this is the place he started for.
His gestures mean to say, *No matter,
I will not oppose your kindness or stay
estranged or go away from you ever.*

We overcome nothing, nothing overcomes us.
We are children of the air,
no longer do we wish to come down,
singly, in pairs, in troops, in tribes,
we ride through air, we are carried everywhere.
We overcome nothing, nothing overcomes us.

We pass through space, space passes through us,
unaltered, undisturbed. We do not touch,
obstruct no light, do not lift the dust
or stir the moonbeam's silver motes.
We pass, and nothing has passed.
We overcome nothing, nothing overcomes us.

Space is our manna, we grow spacious,
thin as the air that meets us always
with its surpriseless open stare.
There is always more and no one to thank.
As it comes, we take it and move on.
We overcome nothing, nothing overcomes us.

Do not think us sad, we do not think
we are sad. We are gentle. We do not care.
The wind comes and combs our voices smooth
as it does our hair. Our voices stream away.
Hear!, now, far off, they disappear,
and off, farther off, appear to appear.

We overcome nothing, nothing overcomes us.

In the flat cosmic suburbs
beyond Altair, there
too they decant and sip, space
is a continuous seething
of lively chatter that is
very much our lively chatter.
And in the suburbs beyond
beyond-Altair, beyond
everywhere, in fact, the same
tinkling and telephones, the same
closing of frigidaires,
a generous hubbub of voices
like our voices,
the same odor and press of persons.

The last last vacancy
has been filled, and far off
the grains of space tip
and drift toward us, bumping
into others not unlike,
and now there is someone
who arrives at the party
just a little late,
garbling apologies,
glass in hand, a trifle high,
to be sure, looking
like the neighbor next-door
and saying that "out there"
is "in here," that
really nothing is beyond,
nothing that is not ourselves,
since the universe is us.

Space leaks through the floor,
and goes on to other
parties on other stars
that are, of course,
the same parties,
the same stars.
In the spacelessness where we are
as we are,
oh, beautifully immanent,
buzzing, swarming, completely
in touch with everything,
we raise glasses and voices
and rapidly say all
the names of which we can
think, to toast
whatever it is
is missing our lives.

Come look at the girls, said Edward
from the window, *rue Gît-le-Coeur*.
They ran to look.
Storeys down, some black queens
stood shrieking in the street. Then
the burble of Paul's tolerant chuckle
accompanied their disfigured joy; then
two Arab boys drifting through the flat
as through remembered desert, it was
as dry almost, as dusty as that.
At noon another—ex-student of
the medical fac—could be seen
waking in a farther room: Someone
Anodymene washed up among
the dingy rivulets of a sheet,
rubbing sleep-sand from his eyes
with fragile dirty fists.
Half-old-pasha, half-mama,
Edward pottered in a tattery robe,
emptied ashtrays, vaguely dishragged
a table, childlike handed 'round
bits of Dada curios in polyglot,
clippings, photos, collages of
outmoded monsters, broken, twisted limbs.
Someone said it made him think
of shreds of Greeks hanging, heaped
in the cyclops' cloaca-eye-and-maw,
the roaring cave's dark doorway. Speaking
of Greeks, Paul, tamping his pipe
with a scorched thumb and puffing, explained
about the war between the gods of earth,
the gods of air, the former smouldering,

blasphemous, full of spite, the latter
quick, arrogant, deceitful, thundering.
Was this place a pinnacle or hell?
Babel, perhaps. Hell on high.
Now we could smell the darkness in our light.
At two, the psychoanalyst from Lódź
came in, years and years out of Auschwitz,
a neo-nihilist loaded with matches
from the holocaust. Little flames
leaped from his coat, from everywhere
about him, his eyes gleamed, his forest hands
rubbed cracklingly together and he laughed,
certain that nothingness would be
preceded by fire, and every brilliant
horror have its utterly dark sabbath.
In that faith, he glanced around the room
and rested.

The tones are pure,
                    but in his mouth, too much
too long in use, you hear the surging gangs
of children at their grimy murderous game.
They kick up dirt with their heels; they shout, defy,
accuse, drop to a knee and take deadly aim
while their stuttering throats slam bullets out;
when they win, joy careens and smashes through them
like a speeding car out of control; defeated,
they bluster and brood, deflate, droop; they cheat
too often; caught, they jut their jaws, grab for more;
they moralize, they give the raspberry, the finger,
they whisper, mutter, backbite, consume, secrete,
they swear and forswear and bear false witness;
their bickering and deliberate quarrels
wreck the game; furiously, they begin over,
hurl themselves into play with the abandon
of bursting pods; they scatter; they change sides
with swift and passionate righteousness.

Meanwhile, he is singing away
as if there's no such thing as history.
His eyes roll up for the high notes in little
mimicries, he stands on his toes.
The butterfly blue heavens escape
the mile-high nets, something
flickers on the heights, something
not itself not anything else
disappears.
              Down
in the mouth, wanting
to shove the kids aside,

his tongue flops fuzzily,
caterpillar from the green leaf blown.
It's all *bel canto* and mucky shoes.
You can taste every lozenge he ever sucked.
Gallons in the salons.
Mouthwash carbona cologne beer steam starch.
The fraying vocal apparatus in the closet
is an old waiter's black suit:
stiff with habit, stands at attention, knees
bent, hand held out, pockets distended;
one cuff in the soup, one foot in the gravey;
worm wants it; dog
daunts it; cat kittens on it.
Song?
He mourns mewfully.

If only the world had one unadvertised pleasure!
—and one unmentionable terror!
and one note free of every melody!
he could spit those children out and shut the shop
and live happily humming till millennium comes,
should anything be worth the saving.

Afterward, the cherubim:
blazing wind machines, tall trumpets
imperative at the four corners.
Fanfare over fanfare, as if
the curtain might never stop
going up—for years it blew like that.
Then, in their high rustling heads,
a thousandfolded emptiness
shivered darkly through the leaves,
and under a burnished sun, before
a sky washed clear, hung up to dry,
scenes from the new life drifted over
the blank lustrous curve of their eyes.
Above, in ivory robes, with fixed
misanthropic eyes and beaks, the troop
of prophets, long rows in the air, were
opening, closing mouths, still saying
Better heart-attack than heartbreak,
saying Indignation never pity.
Suddenly, cherubim were gone.
In all directions, the prophets saw
sunny miles of empty metropoli,
—the zombiverse.
It was so quiet you could
have heard your heart stop.
They called this the new beginning,
the second chance.
Later, they went into a dead beer garden
and broke out vintage stuff, from before
the flood. Water had gotten to it
and new mouths maybe can hardly taste

old wine, but it felt good
somehow to sit around
in the sun of the year one
and pledge with vinegar and mud,
thin and sour like nostalgia,
gritty with our offended clay.

They hurry, they take
their utensils, their little
gods with them;
now light
throngs the empty sill,
this purity being
looked through by sunny
lane, by sand, by
unmeaning chop and lilt
of waters.
In the carts
the potted cactus, the
geraniums, the broken
drum and frying pan
and little creaking
chair jolt forward
into exile in
their usual ecstasy
of self-perception.
No one any longer
looks back, and burning,
quick to restore
the empty realm,
leaps to the window dancing.

No longer troubling to charm, curt,
without cadence, they bark their lies,
impatient of our credulity,
like teachers who repeat the lesson
for idiots stuck on the first page.
They pity themselves, complain
our stupidity forces them to lie,
and say, *Why can't we do as we please?*

Their guile, complaints, their greediness.
Capable of nurture only, we
are like mothers, we nourish them,
believe what they say and repeat it
for one another, knowing the while
credulity isn't enough
and something not easy is required,
a pretense of intelligence,
a sacrifice, a faith they could believe
worthy of their treachery, worth
betraying. It is adversaries they crave,
and what lies we think we hear are
higher truths we have overheard.
                              But nights,
the children sitting in a ring, we take up
the papers, speak aloud the pathos
and mystery of our leaders' lives.
Alone in dark chambers, in ordinary-
seeming chairs, at the innermost recession
of a thousand thoughts, they reach decisions,
while wives bring warmth and grace and wit
(we venerate their warmth and grace and wit)
when they are tired or under the weather,

servants trot softly in the hallways
with urgent whispers, vehement faces,
and only with the utmost diffidence
their dogs roll over—lips in rictus,
eyes alert, little paws held up like sticks
—begging to have their bellies scratched.
To know this is a constant pleasure!
Then, to move our coarse fingers along the lines,
over the inscrutable words, to murmur their names,
to feel our gross lips fumbling their names,
to feel ourselves becoming more human,
to draw close about the fire!
                    At such moments,
overcome by shame for our clamorous natures,
we look down, our eyes seek out the children,
we see their small heads, unimaginably
like ours, bent above the pages, the furious
concentration that grips their innocent
unblemished faces, their minds that leap ahead
to seize the ending before the tale is done.
This generation, we say to ourselves,
they will be different, *they* will be better!
Powerfully, they bend our eyebeams to themselves
—we see, we *feel* them bending within
our unbreakable domestic circle.
This is awesome, this is more than sweet.
And what would life be without affection!
—it is our solace, our achievement,
it is the language we speak.
It says that everything is true.
And truly, as we disbelieve less, the world
becomes miraculous beyond believing,
though less a place requiring us, less, at last,
our own.
                    The thought of our nonentity,

the world without us, this large bare ball
flying empty into the empty day,
is stunning, takes our breath, like something
intimate and alien, like a knife
in the lungs.
        Our leaders chide us,
for sentimental, for living in others,
but can they guess our helplessness?
We break another stick from the ramparts
and thrust it on the fire set blazing
by all the power of our affection
—and another necessary lie comes
quiet from the matterless night, settles
panting beside us, warms a bloody muzzle
between paws, snuggles down toward sleep.
So everything ends, like this, near a fire
in silence and wonder, our fingers idly
soothing a murderer's nape, and somewhere
out there, a last bitter scream doesn't stop.
They don't bother stifling it,
even with a lie.

The winter night gives birth before me, it is you
hurrying from the mists of Lyon
between the New Hotel and Place Carnot:
shock of dullish hair, widow's peak,
dead uncle's baggy suit, dead nephew's
bursting coat, dirty collar, varicose tie,
suitcase so torn you've webbed it with cord.
In broken French you ask for the bus to Bordeaux.
In broken French I answer, crying out,
That way, sir! with confident misdirection,
never dreaming you'll go, yet off you rush,
limping grandly, swinging your free elbow.
What business could *you* ever have in Bordeaux?
Might as well ask for the bus to Budapest,
the bus to Chicago! Oslo! Maracaibo!
Why kid me, a stranger in the street, asking
for outlandish places, pretending
a life to live and all that says,
history, property, people, god,
that whole landscape of the arbitrary
to give you breath, to call you darling!

And so you go,
country on your back, selves in a satchel,
a cipher becoming the century.
Powerless, you do nothing, recur,
like a myth, echoing around the corner,
stepping off boldly on the wrong foot
toward the empty provinces of rain.

A BALCONY IN BARCELONA
for Madeleine Morati-Schmitt

I

Space abstracts the body, and the eye,
more avid, reaches toward some clinging point
way way off. But it is the twilight,
gentle and victorious as an undertaker . . .
O there are weeping mysteries here, something
I knew that I've forgot, some creature-thought
yawning its drowsy dim way to the lap
of a little cave. At times like these one feels
suddenly one has misplaced the whole sky.
Now hill and sea are asleep in caves,
and far away the ancient port lights up
and little roads on the slope are lit and go
floating off in the dark immensity.
More, more lights! cries the eye demanding only
the impossible. Grand burial in the air,
the stars in procession—is it my body there,
my eye following it aloft over the city
and over all and on and out of the world?

2

With so much sky there's so much weather. It's
like being at sea, where the day's wind or sun
are a destiny filling all the time till sleep.
"Looks like rain today," which won't be the same
as yesterday's. Today's weather is today's.
There is no other news on the balcony
but what comes drifting down from above, rain
today, tomorrow sun. We're that close to the gods,
who speak in elements and have no other
business but leisurely conversing, charming
the sky with bolts, with clouds, with subtle
pituitary whispers and large vascular
digressions. Our bodies listen, brought always
to the same postures at the railing to gaze
with the same powerful vague intent. Rain
it is today! A rainy day in Barcelona
is all the rainy days the world will ever need.

to Pete Foss,
God give him good berth!

Shipped deckhand June of 'fifty-one
aboard the freighter *Willis Kerrigan,*
chartered to Union Sulphur and Oil
(stack colors dull ochre, black)
and carrying coal from Norfolk out
to Dunkerque, France on the Marshall Plan
—old Liberty de-mothballed in Baltimore,
shaken down, painted over, and papered
with a pickup crew, scourings of the seven
saloons of Hoboken, Mobile, Camden, Pedro.

Here we are, bosun, carpenter, watches. Jake,
Cox, Wally, Slim, Chips, the Finn, myself,
Ole, Moe, Chris the Dane, Pete Foss, bosun,
average sorts of monster, more or less:
brawler or bragger, wino, nut, nag,
bully, slob, simpleton, thief,
this carp of leaden contempt,
this john aspiring to mackerel,
these sponge, crab, clam,
bottom-feeders almost to a man,
lungless on land, finless afloat,
sifting the margin of muck
with sodden sense and cramping gut.
Adrift in wide iron belly
amid tall waves always at world edge,
sailors are liable to misadventure
into monstrosity, forgotten
elsewhere, lost to themselves.
                              Near

mutiny, storms at sea, quarreling
drunks, fistfights, a broken screw, two
stowaways, a crewman's fiddle stolen, heaved
overboard or hocked, kangaroo court and Moe
condemned to dine alone for dirtiness,
Wally of the middle watch busting open
lockers, out three days slugging hair tonic,
shaving lotion, as if the stuff were scotch,
Lulu and a second whore clambering
over the barges and hustled below
before the ship had ever touched a dock.
These the adventures, nothing legendary,
just "adventures," nothing more, anecdotes
from someone else's less-than-war.
                              Otherwise,
our common peaceable humanity's
old routine: chipping gunwale rust
soogeeing the wheelhouse down, bow watch
under the stars, the coffee pot perking
day and night, the binnacle's hypnotic
click-click-click, meals and meals, cards
in the mess, Pete Foss' lined face pokered
around his pipe, sunning out on the hatches,
winch work, fire drill, boat drill,
endless talk of sex, endless trivial
housekeeping chores of homeless householders
wandering on the wide wide sea, sleep
in the throbbing, rolling, roaring, yawing, shivering tub.

Each from his isolation, each
from transmogrification,
his little pleasure
or lengthy sleep,
a sudden gracing woke;
the mast, our common labor,

46

a confluence of task and wave,
of waves blown into wind,
the one the pure transparent day
brought us there together.
At the infinitesimal inter-
section of these historic enterprises,
commercial, national, imperial,
within an indefinable cosmic
context, six of us climbed the mainmast
with beaknosed hammers, buckets of paint
to scrape it clean, to make it new.
Gulls dove, dolphins rolled,
sun swam ahead on the sea,
and we wind-jockeys on bosun chairs
in our thrilled community
let lines go and flew, out around
the dancing lodgepole of the turning sky
that first and dazzling morning of the world.

So it happens
when Messiah stands
among us, this lost relation,
a small, forgotten cousin
from the other side who looks
with eager puzzlement into
our faces he half-recognizes,
half-guesses from the photo
he carries. Touchingly, with
wonder and disappointment,
he says, "It isn't you, Marsha,
Judy, Sam! Why am I always
lost and lose my way to
the appointed heart?" and goes off
while we cry out, "Mistake!
we are the very ones, look again,
seek us still in ourselves!"
—and yearn indeed to become
those pure incalculable names.

She says, "Bembú"* (my surname, cognomen,
Panache, alas!), "poet named too well for lies,
Get out! I will not look at you again!"
She climbs the haughty tower of her wrath
And with a final imprecation casts

Herself naked on the roaring wind.
Dido reigning amid the raging populace
Of her pyre was not half so glorious
As you are stamping your foot on the floor.
My anger fizzles, admiration flares.

By the sainted mother who bore you,
Your worthy uncles and lamented father,
Solid men of esteemed position,
Merchants all of Iberian delicacies
And local products of the highest caliber

Sold in two suburban branches
And in the main store off the Plaza,
O redolent heiress of Park Provisions,
Pensive or busy at the counter
In the cool green depths among the jars

Of saffron, cinnamon, and chili peppers,
The monster cheeses, the Asturian *cidra,*
The pickled parts of *toros de lidia,*
And tins with scrollworked, gilded labels,
Fine testimonia of kings (kings in exile

Or dead long since from natural causes,

* Fat lips.

Whose fluttering spirits haunt, blue ribbon
In a bluer hand, the fairs of a fairer day)
—Reflect on those dusty lightless monarchs,
Their proper queens alongside thinking hard

Of dignity and their estates, their skirts
Of stone on stoney knees, their consorts,
Loyal in death, loveless and unappealing!
And do not suffer your lovely ear's abuse
By what those whisperers impute to me!

As I respect your blessed mother,
Your uncles and the family business,
The lace that hems your bourgeois slip,
The droplets gleaming on your tender lids
While you complete the inventory

Or verify a bill of lading, know
If I could tell you in my voice itself
And not in this impersonation,
I would say I love you all
Beyond approach or approximation.

That I am Bembú, bohemian, poet,
Posturing vainly in the public face,
Have given all my sighs for publication
And your heavenly tears to the dreadful cheeks
Of poetry readers—forgive me, *nena!*,

For I cannot, yet cannot change my purposes.
And what is any other but a pale
And seeable moon burning with the beauty
Of your almond eyes so fierce and sweet
I am blinded if I look one minute!

Too timid to be Homer, for all my mad
Ambition, brightening his night with song
Singing *that* denied his eyes' possession,
I glance aside. The meager sights
Starve my eyes' continual craving.

That flaming day they took you from me
In their shiny flatulent car, the gloomy
Folk of your family crammed among,
You continued smiling with exceeding
Joy, my heart has not altered to this day.

Wait for me at noon before the store
And I shall escort you in the streets
Of gossips who joylessly contest with tongues,
Those files of envy scraping harmlessly
As cricket legs on the gates of heaven.

We will go the long way 'round, and by
The roundest way return. You shall be seen
To take my arm, I to incline my head.
By these signs we shall be known
Those unknowable noons when the star

Is burning and stillness both
And both in our sufficing shade.

*Translated from the Spanish of
Juan Díaz Bembú, born in
Morovis, Puerto Rico, in 1933.*

THE TWO

Hidden everywhere,
they are two, are
twins, are husband wife,
scrolls turning to offer,
turning to take, and lie
in gradual quiet speaking,
asleep and waking together,
waking to one another
at night, both one and
divided, sky and earth,
beginning end. How
strange! how near! they say,
the one and the other,
Be my light, be
my darkness, my sleep,
my waking!
I will!
I am!

Conceit is not news,
vanity not news,
nor the jaunty cripples of a season,
impresarios to their famous
lyrical humps.
        And yet
these thoughts keep me awake, or I
awake to keep such thoughts,
insomnia striving
between shame and envy, saved
by neither from neither, between
nihilism and indignation,
beleaguered by both.

But there you are
with a mailing list and three forgotten volumes,
your toe in the door of forty,
faithful to failure—childhood's eternal
province,—hard times' new hero
in a last corner of the old place,
sniffing the ancient culture of spilt milk,
living lean in a fat time,

my friend,
of indefinite gestures
that wave the light away,
of smiles of stymied gentleness,
of patient carbons,
your black virgins going gray
but keeping in touch,
and puns that go nowhere punctually,
obsolete timetables

of your misery,
your autumn anthologies
shuffling the loose leaves,
your little flame,
your sadness,
your embarrassed tongue,
old porter fumbling bags,
all unspeakably too much to bear.
You gaze out, and nothing there
dissuades you from your privacy.

S.,
it tempers my mind to think of you,
your tiny vortex, its peaceful dwelling
like water on a drain, dauntless
and quiet, spinning, creative, stooping
to scan the humblest darkness
with diffident clarity;
you are gentle and do not weary
and persist for failure, carrying
your small debris around
and around—the lightest things
the deluge left—and you drop
toward its deeper issue, imagining
the earth's unenunciated
still there where your paradise drowned,
the tribe of lost aboriginals,
thick, buried deep, dumb roots
in a place of restoration.

And so you put children together,
wittily, out of whatever: scraps
you find or rummage in the street,
recollecting these neglected,
the tiniest leavings—bits of stone,

bits of metal, glass, and wood.
And topplingly you pile up your solemn
statuary. They stand there waiting,
each two-inch child alone in space,
hundreds and hundreds, a millennium
of foundlings in a falling world,

you down there
barely breathing in Brooklyn,
buried 'live and flinging up
your daily bucket.
The coprophages of success
in the poses of pride, corruption, and wrath
caper on the earth.
You grope in darkness, they grovel in light.

The evening sleeps that stars
may be conceived—see,
they shine, the infant worlds!
How simple that was,
to sleep to the naming
of stars! You slept,
and speech was born in light,
the infant words,
how simple then was!

Come, says happiness,
that anachronism, naming
you and taking your hand
to follow to its early
country. What pleasure now
to see yourself by glow
and fulguration, to be
the star that is here
and star that is there,
the leap and light
—dawn, transparent star!